MW00682454

. . . .

From

. . . .

Date

. . . .

© 2011 by Barbour Publishing, Inc.

ISBN 978-1-61626-405-5

Jokes are compiled from *The 365-Day Clean Joke Book* published by Barbour Publishing Inc.

Published by Barbour Publishing, Inc., P.O. Box 719, Uhrichsville, Ohio 44683, www.barbourbooks.com

Our mission is to publish and distribute inspirational products offering exceptional value and biblical encouragement to the masses.

Member of the
Evangelical Christian
Publishers Association

Printed in China.

365
JOKES
to Brighten Your Day!

BARBOUR
PUBLISHING

Day 1

Little Johnny was bothered with a question that he had to ask his Sunday school teacher.

"Miss Davis, are there any animals in heaven?"

"I'm not sure, Johnny," his teacher responded.

"Well, I just wanted to know, 'cause last Sunday we sang about 'Gladly the Cross-Eyed Bear.'"

Day 2

Sunday School Definitions

Definitions given by children
in a Sunday school class:

Conversion:
"The point after a touchdown."

Fast days:
"The days you have to eat in a hurry."

Epistle:
"The wife of an apostle."

Day 3

Little Ears

A young husband and wife invited their pastor for Sunday dinner. While they were in the kitchen preparing the meal, their young son was in the living room entertaining the pastor.

"What are we having for dinner?" the minister asked.

"Goat," replied the boy.

"Goat?" repeated the startled pastor. "Are you sure about that?"

"Yep," said the youngster. "I heard Dad tell Mom, 'Might as well have the old goat for dinner today as any other day.'"

Day 4

Stuffed Animals

What did the teddy bear say
when he was offered dessert?

"No thanks, I'm stuffed."

Day 5

Airline Safety

It was Johnny Carson who asked
this thought-provoking question:

"If airline travel is so safe, how come
flight attendants sit right next
to the emergency exit?"

Day 6

Fairy-Tale Athletes

Why wasn't Cinderella
good at sports?

Because she had a pumpkin
as her coach!

Day 7

The Wicked Witch

What color hair did the
Wicked Witch of the West have?

Brewnette.

Day 8

BC Fraud

An archaeologist found a coin dated 62 BC and immediately declared it a fraud. How did he know it wasn't real?

BC stands for "Before Christ." This dating system wasn't used until after Christ had been born.

Day 9

What Does a Ring Bear Do?

Little Tony was in his uncle's wedding. As he came down the aisle during the ceremony, he carefully took two steps then stopped and turned to the crowd. When facing the congregation he put his hands up like claws and roared loudly. So it went, step, step, turn, roar, step, step, turn, roar. The congregation was near tears from laughing. By the time little Tony reached the altar, he was near tears, too.

When later asked what he was doing, the boy sniffed and said, "I was being the ring bear."

Day 10

Blame Game

"Mommy, Randall just broke
the bedroom window!"

"Oh no! How did that happen?"

"I threw a shoe at him,
and he ducked."

Day 11

Trade-Ins

Jon: "My parents just got a new computer for my teenage sister."

Ron: "I wish my parents could make that kind of trade for my big sister."

Day 12

Driving Distractions

Ole got a new cell phone, and
on his way home on the freeway,
he called his wife, Lena.

"Hello, Lena. I'm calling you from the
freeway on my new cell phone."

Lena said, "Be careful, Ole. The radio
says that some nut is driving
the wrong way on the freeway."

Ole said, "One nut, my eye.
There are hundreds of them!"

Day 13

_____

Driving Definitions

Low mileage:
What you get when your
car won't start.

Steering committee:
A panel of individuals who aren't
capable of driving by themselves.

Day 14

Driving with Dad

One day a father was driving with his five-year-old daughter when he honked his car horn by mistake.

"I did that by accident," he said.

"I know that, Daddy," she replied.

"How did you know that?"

"Because you didn't holler at the other driver after you honked it."

Day 15

Disney Spells

Patient: "Doctor, sometimes when I wake up in the morning I think I'm Donald Duck; other times I think I'm Mickey Mouse."

Doctor: "How long have you had these Disney spells?"

Day 16

Curious Keys

What keys can't open locks?

Monkeys, donkeys, and turkeys.

Day 17

- - - - - -

Doctor's Handwriting

A pharmacist was squinting and holding the prescription slip up to the light. Finally, she took up a magnifier in a futile effort to read it.

"We don't think too highly of this particular doctor," she told the customer, "but there's one thing he obviously can do better than anyone else on the planet."

"What's that?"

"Read his own handwriting!"

Day 18

Famous Words

The students had behaved abominably at an assembly program, and at the end, the school principal announced sternly that there would be no outdoor recess for the remainder of the week. As he turned from the podium, from the middle of the crowded assembly hall came a shout:
"Give me liberty, or give me death!"

"Who said that?" demanded the principal, wheeling about.

There was a short silence.
Then another anonymous voice called out,
"Patrick Henry?"

Day 19

Class Questions

Teacher: "Can anyone tell me why the Capitol in Washington has a rotunda?"

Student: "So our politicians can run around in circles."

Day 20

A Sherlock Holmes Education

Where did Sherlock Holmes go to school?

Elementary, my dear Watson.

Day 21

Arithmetic Problems

Teacher: "If you had one dollar and you asked your father for another, how many dollars would you have?"

Boy: "One dollar."

Teacher: "Sorry, you don't know your arithmetic."

Boy: "You don't know my father."

Day 22

Nerves of Steel

An ironworker nonchalantly walked the narrow beam fifteen floors above the city sidewalk. Even though a hurricane was blowing and heavy rain was falling, the worker exhibited no fear and was foot-perfect. When he came down to the sidewalk, a man who had been watching him from ground level went over to him and said, "I was really impressed watching you up there. You were so calm. How did you get a job like this?"

"Well, as a matter of fact," replied the ironworker, "I used to drive a school bus, until my nerves gave out."

Day 23

Knock-Knock, Stew

Knock-knock.

Who's there?

Irish Stew.

Irish Stew who?

Irish stew would stay for dinner.

Day 24

Knock-Knock, Ben-Hur

Knock-knock.

Who's there?

Ben Hur.

Ben Hur who?

Ben Hur an hour an' she ain't in sight.

Day 25

- - - - - - -

Noah's Vocation

What did Noah do for a living?

He was an ark-itect.

Day 26

Speeding Pastors

When a traffic cop pulled over
Pastor Johnson for speeding,
the minister reminded the officer,
"Blessed are the merciful,
for they shall obtain mercy."

The cop handed the minister
the ticket and quoted,
"Go thou and sin no more."

Day 27

The Perfect Marriage

He didn't have to listen to her talk
about men she knew before him,
and she didn't have to put up
with his mother.

HAHA ◎ HAHA ◎ HAHA ◎ HAHA ◎ HAHA ◎ HAH

Day 28

Shark Lesson

Boy: "Could you sell me a shark?"

Pet shop owner: "Why do you want a shark?"

Boy: "My cat keeps trying to eat my goldfish, and I want to teach him a lesson."

HAHA ◎ HAHA ◎ HAHA ◎ HAHA ◎ HAH

Day 29

Salesmanship

Computer Spokesperson:
"This computer will do half
your work for you"

Customer: "Then I'll take two!"

Day 30

Mozart's Chickens

Why did Mozart sell his chickens?

They kept saying, "Bach, Bach, Bach."

Day 31

Bulletin Blooper

"Ushers will swat latecomers
at these points in the service."

Day 32

Checks and Frying Pans

A lady sent the following letter
to a mail-order house:
"Gentlemen: Please send me
the frying pan on page 10 of your
catalog. If it's any good, I'll send you
$14.95 by return mail."

The reply came back:
"Madam: Please send us your check
for $14.95. If it's any good, we'll send
you the frying pan by return mail."

Day 33

- - - - -

Patience

An angler looked up from the stream
and spoke to the man sitting
above him on the bank:

"You've been sitting there watching
me fish for two hours now.
Why don't you just fish yourself?"

"Ain't got the patience for it."

Day 34

The Prima-Donna Quarterback

"I like the statistics of your quarterback, Evans," a pro scout told a college football coach. "What's your opinion of him personally?"

"Good skills. Sort of a prima donna, though."

"How do you mean?"

"Well, let's just say when he makes a big play, he's a big advocate of the idea of taking personal responsibility for the way things happen. When he gets sacked, he's a big advocate of the concept of luck."

Day 35

Fish Out of Water

In what country can fish
survive out of water?

Finland.

Day 36

Math on a Boat

A boat has a ladder that has six rungs.
Each rung is one foot apart.
The bottom rung is one foot from the
water. The tide rises at twelve inches
every fifteen minutes.
High tide peaks in one hour.
When the tide is at its highest,
how many rungs are underwater?

None. The boat rises with the tide.

Day 37

Shipwrecked Food

What can you always find
to eat if you're shipwrecked
on a desert island?

Lots of SAND-wiches.

Day 38

True Love

Wife: "Do you love me just because my father left me a fortune?"

Husband: "Not at all, darling. I would love you no matter who left you the money."

Day 39

A Pet Skunk

"Mom, I want a pet skunk," said Tricia.

"And where, exactly, do you propose to keep it?"

"In my brother's room."

"What would he do about the terrible odor?"

"I'm sure the skunk's used to it."

Day 40

Fierce Mosquitoes

Some Boy Scouts were on a camping trip. The mosquitoes were so fierce, the boys had to hide under their blankets to avoid being bitten.

Then one of the Scouts saw some lightning bugs and said, "We might as well give up. They're coming after us with flashlights."

Day 41

Charged by the Question

Scotty: "Are you a lawyer?"

Attorney: "Yes."

Scotty: "How much do you charge?"

Attorney: "A hundred dollars for four questions."

Scotty: "Isn't that awfully expensive?"

Attorney: "Yes. What's your fourth question?"

Day 42

- - - - - -

Friday Afternoons

One CEO always scheduled
staff meetings for four thirty on
Friday afternoons.
When one of the employees
finally got up the nerve to ask why,
the CEO explained,
"I'll tell you why—it's the only time
of the week when none of you seems
to want to argue with me."

Day 43

Trips to Rome

A pizza shop owner was audited
by the IRS. The agent said, "You have
some travel expenses that need to
be explained. How do you justify
four trips to Rome this year?"

"Oh, I don't need to justify that,"
replied the shop owner. "Don't you
know? We deliver."

Day 44

AM Radio

Art: "Did you hear the concert
on the radio last night?"

Keri: "My radio won't
come on at night."

Art: "What's wrong with it?"

Keri: "It's an AM radio."

Day 45

- - - - - -

Baggage Destinations

A man at the airline counter told the woman behind the desk, "I'd like this bag to go to London, this one to Seattle, and this one to Quebec."

"I'm sorry, sir. We can't do that," she replied.

"I'm sure you can," he answered. "That's what you did the last time I flew with you."

Day 46

Prescription

"I've had horrible indigestion
for the past two days," a patient said.

"And what have you been doing for it?"
asked the doctor.

"Taking an antacid twice a day
and drinking nothing but milk,"
said the patient.

"Good—exactly what I would have
suggested myself. That'll be fifty dollars."

Day 47

Pasta Diet

"Have you heard about the amazing new pasta diet?"

"No. What's involved?"

"It's so simple! You simply learn to walk pasta da refrigerator without stopping—and pasta da cookie jar and pasta da cupboard...."

Day 48

- - - - - -

Auto Mechanic in Surgery

An auto mechanic in the hospital was chatting nervously with his surgeon while being prepped for an operation. "Sometimes I wish I'd gone into your line of work," he told the doctor. "Everything you doctors do is so cut and dried and tidy. With me, I spend half a day taking an engine apart and putting it back together, and it seems I always have a couple of parts left over."

"Yes," said the surgeon. "I know the feeling."

Day 49

Good News?

A rural mail carrier at the end of
World War II took the news of the
armistice to an isolated mountain family. He
thought the good tidings would bring smiles,
but the woman on the porch shook her
head sadly. "I s'pose it figures," she grumbled.

"What do you mean?"
asked the carrier.

"We sent our Jeb off to join
the army two months ago."

"Looks like he missed all the fightin'."

"That's what I mean. That boy
never could hold a job."

Day 50

Synonym Spelling

Teacher: "George, please tell the class what a synonym is."

George: "A synonym means the same thing as the word you can't spell."

Day 51

Modern Art

A third-grade class went to an art museum. The students were instructed to sit and wait until the guide was ready to begin the tour. Two boys, however, decided to explore on their own. They walked down a hallway and entered a room filled with modern art pieces.

"Quick, run," said one, "before they say we did it!"

Day 52

Snow Day

It had been snowing for several hours when an announcement came over the college campus intercom: "Will the students who are parked on University Drive please move their cars promptly? We must begin plowing."

Fifteen minutes later, there came another announcement: "Will the nine hundred students who went to move thirty-four cars please return to class?"

Day 53

Mark 17

One Sunday morning Pastor Bob advised his congregation, "Next week I plan to preach about the sin of lying. In preparation for my message, I want you all to read Mark 17."

The following Sunday the reverend asked for a show of hands from those who had read Mark 17. Every hand went up. Pastor Bob smiled and announced, "Well, Mark has only sixteen chapters. I will now proceed with my sermon on the sin of lying."

Day 54

You Might Be a Preacher If…

You've been told to get a real job.

You've been tempted to name
your fishing boat *Visitation*.

You couldn't sell used cars.

You said, "I'm NEVER going
to be a preacher!"

You win a door prize at the church
banquet, and people say it was rigged.

Your belly is ever referred to
as "chicken coop."

Your kids nickname you
"Our Father Who Art at a Meeting."

Day 55

Edible Caterpillars

"Are caterpillars good to eat?"
asked a little boy at the dinner table.

"No," said his father. "Why would you
ask a question like that?"

"Well, there was one in your salad,
but it's gone now."

Day 56

The Magician's Parrot

A magician worked on a cruise ship with his pet parrot. The parrot always ruined his act by saying things like, "The card was up his sleeve!" or "The dove was in his pocket!"

One day the ship sank, and the magician and the parrot found themselves adrift on a lifeboat. For a couple of days, they just sat there looking at each other. Finally, the parrot broke the silence and said, "Okay, I give up. What did you do with the ship?"

Day 57

Directions to Heaven

The Reverend Billy Graham tells
of a time early in his ministry when
he arrived in a small town to preach a
revival meeting. Wanting to mail
a letter, he asked a young boy where
the post office was. When the boy
had told him, Dr. Graham thanked him
and said, "If you'll come to the church
this evening, you can hear me give
directions on how to get to heaven."

"I don't think I'll be there," the boy
replied. "You don't even know how
to get to the post office."

Day 58

Hockey Injury

Andy came to work limping like crazy. One of his coworkers noticed and asked Andy what happened.

"Oh, nothing," Andy replied. "It's just an old hockey injury that acts up once in a while."

"Gee, I never knew you played hockey," the coworker responded.

"I don't," explained Andy. "I hurt it last year when some stupid official put my favorite player in the penalty box. I put my foot through the television screen."

Day 59

Basketball Gym

Why did the basketball team
flood the gymnasium?

It was the only way they could
sink any baskets.

Day 60

Responses to the Question,
"How Is Business?"

Tailor: "Oh, it's sew-sew."

Electrician: "It's fairly light."

Author: "All write."

Farmer: "It's growing."

Astronomer: "Looking up!"

Elevator operator:
"Well, it has its ups and downs."

Trash collector: "It's picking up."

Day 61

Execution Choices

A murderer is condemned to death,
but he is allowed to choose how
he will be executed. The first choice
is to be burned at the stake,
the second to be shot by firing squad,
and the third to be given over to lions
that haven't eaten in two years.
Which choice is the best?

The third.
Lions that haven't eaten
in two years are dead.

Day 62

Musical Lines

Mozart: "What did the Terminator say to Beethoven?"

Brahms: "Tell me."

Mozart: " 'I'll be Bach!' "

Day 63

Wrong Number

A teenage girl had to stay at her girlfriend's overnight. She was unable to call her parents until the next morning. "Mom, it's Caroline. I'm fine. My car broke down last night, and by the time I got to Julie's house it was well past midnight. I knew it was too late to call. Please don't be mad at me!" By now, the woman at the other end of the phone realized the caller had the wrong number.

"I'm sorry," she said, "I don't have a daughter named Caroline."

"Oh Mom! I didn't think you'd be this mad!"

Day 64

Computer Classes

Did you hear about the spider
that enrolled in computer courses?

It wanted to learn how
to design web pages.

Day 65

The Perfect Watch

Mack paid 650 dollars for his gold
watch. It was rustproof, shockproof,
magnetic proof, fireproof,
and, of course, waterproof.
There was only one thing
wrong with it:

He lost it.

Day 66

Surgeon's Mask

Why do surgeons wear masks
during an operation?

So that if any mistake is made,
no one will know who did it.

Day 67

Dying Democrat

A dying man told his wife he wanted
to join the Democratic Party. All his life
he'd been a staunch Republican, and his
wife wondered why he felt the sudden
change in political bent in his final days.

His logic: "I want it to be them
losing a voter, not us."

Day 68

Library Books

Student: "I'd like to check out this book on blood clots."

Librarian: "I'm sorry; that doesn't circulate."

Day 69

Knock-Knock, Butcher

Knock-knock.

Who's there?

Butcher.

Butcher who?

Butcher hands up! This is a robbery!

Day 70

Wedding Mix-Up

Reverend Walker was scheduled to perform a special wedding ceremony immediately following the Sunday morning service. He planned to perform the rite before the entire congregation, but for the life of him, he could not remember the names of the two members whom he was to marry. He got around his dilemma this way: "Will those who want to get married now, please come stand before me?"

At once, six single ladies, four widows, and five single men stood, went to the aisle, and walked to the front.

Day 71

Leaving Eden

What excuse did Adam give to his children as to why he no longer lived in Eden?

"Your mother ate us out of house and home."

Day 72

One Smart Cat

My cat is so smart.
He eats cheese then waits at the
mouse hole with baited breath.

Day 73

An Elephant and a Parrot

What would you get if you crossed
a parrot with an elephant?

An animal that tells you
everything it remembers.

Day 74

Antique: An item your grandparents bought, your parents got rid of, and you're buying again.

Argument: A fight over who can get in the last word first.

Barium: What we do to most people when they die.

Business meeting: A time for people to talk about what they're supposed to be doing.

Confidence: The human quality that comes before experience.

Experience: Something you've acquired after it's too late to do you much good.

Day 75

Monday

A man rode into town on Monday, stayed five days, and then rode out on Monday. How is this possible?

His horse was named Monday.

Day 76

Marine Dentistry

What is the rank of a marine dentist?

Drill sergeant.

Day 77

Great-Grandchildren

A nonagenarian was interviewed
by a local newspaper reporter.

"Do you have a lot of great-
grandchildren?" the reporter asked.

"To tell the truth," confessed the
matriarch, "I expect they're
all pretty ordinary."

Day 78

A mother came inside after gardening
and found a big hole in the middle
of the pie she had made earlier that
morning. She found a gooey spoon
lying in the sink and crumbs all over the
floor. She went to find her son. "David,"
she said, "you promised me that you
wouldn't touch the pie I made.
And I promised you that if you did
touch the pie, I would ground you."

A look of relief came over David.
"Now that I've broken my promise,"
he said, "I think it would be all right
for you to break yours, too."

Day 79

Night Light

What happens when a lightbulb
dresses up in a suit of armor?

He becomes a knight light.

Day 80

Indian Insurance

An elderly man took his faithful but weather-beaten Packard to a tune-up shop for an oil change. The two mechanics exchanged glances as the car puttered to a stop at the garage door.

"Man," said one after emitting a low whistle, "I'll bet that thing's still insured against Indian attack."

Day 81

Car Dealer

Customer: "When I bought this car, you guaranteed that you would fix anything that broke."

Car dealer: "Yes, that's right."

Customer: "Well, I need a new garage."

Day 82

Hearing Aids

An elderly gentleman had serious hearing problems for a number of years. He went to the doctor and was fitted for a set of hearing aids that allowed the man to hear perfectly. The elderly gentleman went back in a month to the doctor, and the doctor said, "Your hearing is perfect. Your family must be really pleased you can hear again."

The gentleman replied, "Oh, I haven't told my family yet. I just sit around and listen to their conversations. I've changed my will five times!"

Day 83

––– ––– ––– ––– –––

One Phone Call

An Amish man in Lancaster County
was arrested because the red lantern
on the back of his buggy blew out.
When he was taken to jail, he was
told he could make one phone call.

But who was he to call?

None of his friends
or family had telephones.

Day 84

Voted "Most Likely to Succeed"

Porcupines: They're sharp.

Fireflies: They're bright.

Rabbits: They're great at multiplying.

Hummingbirds: They finish
their hum-work.

Cats: They get purr-fect grades.

Elephants: They have lots of gray matter.

Day 85

Chemistry Class

The students in the chemistry class were watching the professor give a demonstration of the properties of various acids. "Now," said the professor, "I am going to drop a silver dollar into this glass of acid. Will it dissolve?"

"No, sir," answered one of the students.

"No?" quizzed the professor. "Could you explain to the class why it won't dissolve?"

"Because," the student replied, "if the money would dissolve, then you wouldn't drop it in."

Day 86

Definitions

Graduate school: The approximate point at which a university student ceases dependency on parents and commences dependency on spouse.

Money: A device by which parents stay in touch with their college children.

Day 87

Old-Timers' Sunday

First Baptist has instigated a summer
special day—Old-Timers' Sunday.
This year farmer John Calver brought
in his horse and carriage with
a hand-lettered sign:

ENERGY-EFFICIENT VEHICLE.
RUNS ON OATS AND GRASS.
CAUTION: DO NOT STEP IN EXHAUST.

Day 88

A Straight Face

Pastor father: "I never kissed a girl before I married your mother. Will you be able to tell your children that?"

Parsonage son:
"Not with a straight face."

Day 89

A Stingy Man

A rather stingy man died and went to heaven. He was met at the front gate by Saint Peter, who led him on a house tour down the golden streets. They passed mansion after beautiful mansion until they came to the end of the street and stopped in front of a tiny shack without gold paving in front. "And here is where you will be living, sir," Peter announced.

"Me, live here?" the stingy man yelled. "How come?"

Peter replied, "I did the best I could with the money you sent us."

Day 90

Hunting

What does the lion say
to his friends before they go
out hunting for food?

"Let us prey."

Day 91

Panda Bear

A panda bear walked into a restaurant and ordered a sandwich. When he received the sandwich, he ate it and then took out a gun, shot a hole in the ceiling, and left the restaurant. A policeman caught up with the panda and told him he had broken the law. The panda bear told the policeman that he was innocent, and, if he didn't believe him, to look in the dictionary. The policeman got a dictionary and looked up panda bear.

The entry read,
"Panda Bear: Eats shoots and leaves."

Day 92
- - - - -

Squirrels' Favorite

Which composer is the squirrels'
all-time favorite?

Tchaikovsky.
He wrote *The Nutcracker Suite*.

Day 93

- - - - - -

The Best View

The crowd was mercilessly jeering
and heckling the referee in a high
school match. Finally, the poor official
walked over to the bleachers and sat
down next to his loudest critic.

"What are you doing?"
asked the spectator.

"Well," said the ref, "it seems you
get the best view from here."

Day 94

An Archaeologist's Career

Why did the archaeologist
go bankrupt?

Because his career was in ruins.

Day 95

Main Entrance

A shopkeeper was discouraged
when a new business opened up next
door and erected a huge sign that read,
BEST DEALS.

The shopkeeper was panicked until he
got an idea. He put the biggest sign
of all over his own shop—it read,
MAIN ENTRANCE.

Day 96

- - - - - - -

Once Upon a Time

Once upon a time, there was a clever
thief charged with treason against
the king and sentenced to die.
However, the king decided to be
a little merciful and let the thief
choose which way he would die.
Which way should he choose?

He should choose to die of old age.

Day 97

Zoo Arrest

Frank: "Did you hear about the guy
who was arrested at the zoo
for feeding the pigeons?"

Harry: "No. What's wrong
with feeding the pigeons?"

Frank: "He fed them to the lions."

Day 98

Flying Reservations

A man went to the airline counter.
The ticket agent asked,
"Sir, do you have reservations?"

He replied, "Reservations?
Of course I have reservations,
but I'm flying anyway."

Day 99

Voted "Most Likely to Fail"

Squids: They can't ink straight.

Gorillas: They monkey around too much.

Mice: They just squeak by.

Cows: They copy off each udder.

Turtles: They're always late to class.

Lizards: They are always losing
their newt-books.

Squirrels: They drive the teacher nuts.

Parrots: They keep repeating
their first year.

Day 100

Dean's List

College student: "Hey, Dad! I've got some great news for you!"

Father: "What, son?"

College student: "Remember that five hundred dollars you promised me if I made the dean's list?"

Father: "I certainly do."

College student: "Well, you get to keep it."

Day 101

Humorous Headlines

SUSPECT SAYS HE FIRED GUN
TO FRIGHTEN DECEASED

ELDERLY MAN SLIPS IN BATHTUB,
BREAKS NEW YEAR'S RESOLUTION

CAR HITS JAYWALKER WITH NO HEADLIGHTS

WOMAN EXPECTED TO RECOVER
FROM FATAL CRASH

Day 102

Kittens

A three-year-old went with his dad to see a litter of kittens. On returning home, he breathlessly told his mom there were two boy kittens and two girl kittens. "How did you know which were which?" his mom asked.

"Daddy picked them up and looked underneath," the boy replied.
"I think it's printed on the bottom."

Day 103

Patient Diagnosis

Patient: "Doctor, I don't know what's wrong with me—I hurt all over. If I touch my shoulder here, I hurt, and if I touch my leg here, I hurt, and if I touch my head here, I hurt, and if I touch my foot here, I hurt."

Doctor: "I believe your finger is broken."

Day 104

Health Care Definitions

Acupuncturist: A Chinese doctor
who quietly does his jab.

Hospital: The place to wind up people
who are run down.

Orthodontist: A doctor who
braces children.

Day 105

Marrying a Military Man

Mrs. Green: "My daughter's marrying a military man—a second lieutenant."

Mrs. Gray: "So, she let the first one get away?"

Day 106

Tips to Improve Your Writing

- Avoid alliteration. Always.
- Never use a long word when a diminutive one will do.
- Employ the vernacular.
- Avoid ampersands & abbreviations, etc.
- Parenthetical remarks (however relevant) are unnecessary.
- Remember to never split an infinitive.
- Foreign words and phrases are not apropos.
- One should never generalize.

Day 107

Dating and Marrying

"The difference between dating and marrying," a father advised his college son, "is a matter of expectations."

"What do you mean, Dad?"

"You take your girl out to dinner, for example. She appreciates it. You take your wife out to dinner— she expects it."

Day 108

Attention

Young Miss Jones: "I'm going out
with Joe tonight."

Mama Jones: "Joe again? If you like his
attention so much, why don't
you marry him?"

Young Miss Jones: "Because I like
his attention."

Day 109

The Appropriate Form

A woman had been waiting in line more than an hour at the tax office. "If they didn't give us so much red tape to go through," she fumed to no one in particular, "both the government and the taxpayers would be better off."

A bedraggled clerk overheard the remark and snapped, "If we want your opinion, we will provide you with the appropriate form to complete."

Day 110

Makes Sense to Me

If baby pigs are called piglets,
why aren't baby bulls called bullets
and baby chickens chicklets?

Day 111
- - - - -

Playing Inside

"Oh no! The weather forecaster is calling for rain!" said the kangaroo to the rabbit.

"What's the problem with that?" asked the rabbit. "We could use some rain."

"Yes, but that means my children will have to stay inside to play."

Day 112

American Food Habits

Jay Leno observing the food habits of Americans: "Do you remember when they said movie popcorn is bad for you, and the same for Chinese food? They now say that sandwiches are bad for you because of the high fat content. Anything with mayo, cheese, or meat is bad for you.

Do you realize that all those years when you were a kid and you carried your lunch to school, the Twinkie was probably the healthiest thing in there?"

Day 113

- - - - - - -

Weight Lifting

I don't believe for a second
that weight lifting is a sport.
They pick up a heavy thing and
put it down again.
I call that indecision.

Day 114

Crime

What do you get when you cross
a robber and a shark?

A bite out of crime.

Day 115

Two Caddies

Frank: "Well, Ted, you've certainly come up in the world. You're playing golf with two caddies."

Ted: "Oh, it was my wife's idea."

Frank: "Your wife?"

Ted: "Yeah. She thought I ought to spend more time with the kids."

Day 116

Things You'll Never Hear Your Redneck Cousin Say

"Duct tape won't fix that."

"I thought Graceland was tacky."

"No kids in the back of the pickup; it's not safe."

"I just couldn't find a thing at Walmart today."

"Little Debbie snack cakes have too many saturated fats."

"Hey, here's an episode of *Hee-Haw* that we haven't seen."

"The tires on that truck are too big."

Day 117

Teenage Drivers

Two street people were being entertained watching a teenager try to park a car across the street. The space was ample, but the driver just couldn't maneuver the car into it. Traffic was jammed. Angry drivers honked, further flabbergasting the poor youth. It took a full five minutes before the car was in place.

"That," said one of the idlers, "is what you call paralyzed parking."

Day 118

--- --- --- ---

Santa's Motorcycle

If Santa rode a motorcycle,
what kind would it be?

A Holly Davidson.

Day 119

Jazz Trio

A lady aboard a cruise ship was not
impressed by the jazz trio in one
of the shipboard restaurants.
When her waiter came around,
she asked, "Will they play anything I ask?"

"Of course, madam."

"Then tell them to go play shuffleboard."

Day 120

An Apple a Day

If an apple a day keeps the doctor
away, what will an onion do?

Keep everyone away.

Day 121

Milk Bath

Lisa: "I've heard that a milk bath is good for the skin, so I'll need enough to fill the tub."

Grocer: "Pasteurized?"

Lisa: "No, just up to my chin will do."

Day 122

Single Seat

An overzealous traffic cop stopped a country vicar making his rounds on his bicycle. After checking the bike thoroughly and finding nothing, he had to let the cleric go. "You will never arrest me," declared the vicar, "because God is with me wherever I go."

"Well, then," said the cop, "I'm ticketing you for carrying a passenger on a single-seat vehicle."

Day 123

----- --- -----

Definitions

Bank: A place where you can borrow money—provided you can prove you don't need to.

Best man: The one the bride doesn't marry.

Diplomacy: The art of saying "Nice dog!" until you can get your hands on a stick.

Horse sense: Stable thinking.

Day 124

Whichever Comes First

An NFL running back,
anticipating the new season,
is quoted as saying,
"I want to rush for one thousand
or fifteen hundred yards,
whichever comes first."

Day 125

-- -- -- --

Reading the Future

Manuel: "Do you think anyone can really tell the future with cards?"

Todd: "My mom can. She took a look at my report card and told me exactly what was going to happen when my dad got home."

Day 126

Sunday School Questions

A Sunday school teacher asked
her little students as they were on the
way to the church service, "And why
should we be quiet in church?"

A little girl replied,
"Because people are sleeping."

Day 127

Changing a Lightbulb

How many missionaries does
it take to change a lightbulb?

One—and thirty natives to see the light.

Day 128

- - - - - - -

What Is It?

What's gray on the inside
and clear on the outside?

An elephant in a sandwich bag.

Day 129

RV Privacy

Getting away from their high-stress jobs, May and Trey spend relaxing weekends in their motor home. When they found their peace and quiet disturbed by well-meaning but unwelcome visits from other campers, they devised a plan to assure their privacy. Now when they set up camp, they place this sign on their RV door:

INSURANCE AGENT.
ASK ABOUT OUR TERM-LIFE PACKAGE.

Day 130

Animal Crackers

A little boy returned from grocery shopping with his mom. While his mother put away the groceries, the little boy opened his box of animal crackers and spread them out all over the kitchen table. "What are you doing?" asked his mom.

"The box says you shouldn't eat them if the seal is broken," said the little boy. "I'm looking for the seal."

Day 131

Sleeping Children

"What's the most difficult age
to get a child to sleep regularly?"
a new mother asked an older
veteran of child rearing.

"About seventeen years."

Day 132

Safe Landing

"I've never flown before,"
a nervous old lady told the pilot.

"You will bring me down safely,
won't you?"

"All I can say, ma'am," said the pilot,
"is that I've never left anyone
up there yet!"

Day 133

Airport Labeling

A stout businessman took his suitcase from the luggage ramp at the Fresno airport and huffed to the airline's courtesy desk. "What's the meaning of this?" he demanded, showing the agent the large, red-lettered handling tag tied to his suitcase handle. "I'm well aware of my weight problem, but what right does your airline have to comment on it in public?"

The agent read the tag: FAT. "That," she explained, "is the destination code for this airport."

Day 134

- - - - - - -

Liquids

Doctor: "I want you to drink plenty
of liquids so you'll get over this cold."

Mrs. Martin: "I never drink
anything else."

Day 135

Army Hours

Army Hours

The new army recruits were rousted out of their bunks at 3:30 a.m. "You're wasting the best part of the day already!" screamed the sergeant.

One recruit turned to another and muttered, "It sure doesn't take long to spend the night around here."

Day 136

Invading Sparta

When Philip of Macedon was conquering Greece, he encountered only one stronghold of real resistance: the city of Sparta. Hoping to convince the Spartans to surrender without the loss of more soldiers, he sent a messenger warning of all the ravages that would come if Philip's army had to take the city by force.

Sparta's reply was one word in length: "If."

Impressed by their confidence, Philip left the city alone.

Day 137

History Lesson

History teacher: "Why was George Washington standing in the bow of the boat as the army crossed the Delaware?"

Student: "Because he knew if he sat down, he would have to row."

Day 138

College Education

Father: "I pay your tuition at
the Sorbonne, and when I ask you to
show me what you've learned, you take
me to a fancy restaurant and speak to
the waiter in French. You call this
a valuable education?"

Sam: "Sure, Dad. I told him
to give you the check."

Day 139

A Conscientious Objector

An eighth-grade student was having difficulty completing his homework. Finally he slammed his textbook shut, threw down his pencil, and informed his parents, "I've decided I'm a conscientious objector."

"Why did you decide that?" asked his mother.

"Because wars create too much history!"

Day 140

Grades

Father: "How are your grades, Peter?"

Peter: "They're underwater, Dad."

Father: "What do you mean, underwater?"

Peter: "They're below C level."

Day 141

Sunday School Questions

A Sunday school teacher was
reading a Bible story to her class.
"The man named Lot was warned
to take his wife and flee out of the city,
but his wife looked back
and turned to salt."

A little boy softly asked,
"What happened to the flea?"

Day 142

Chickens and Eggs

Two hens were pecking in the yard
when suddenly a softball came sailing
over the fence, landing a few feet
away from them.

One hen said to the other,
"Will you just look at the ones they're
turning out next door!"

Day 143

A Bulldog's Appetite

A pet-shop owner was trying
to talk Mrs. McClellan into buying a
bulldog for her children.

"Oh, they'll love this little rascal!"
said the clerk. "He's full of fun
and he eats anything. He especially
likes children."

Day 144

A Politician's Speech

The politician concluded a boisterous but shallow speech filled with impossible promises sure to appeal to the particular audience. Mingling with the crowd, he happened on a wise, respected old city father. Hoping for a compliment within hearing of some of the audience, he asked the old man what he thought of the speech.

"Well," the gentleman said thoughtfully, "I think for those who want to hear about those kinds of things, those were exactly the kinds of statements they wanted to hear."

Day 145

The Greatest President

Politician: "Do you know what made
George Washington such
a great president?"

Interviewer: "Sure, he never blamed
any of the country's problems on the
previous administration."

Day 146

Newlywed Dinners

A new bride cooked her first meal for her husband. "My mother taught me to cook, and I can cook two things well— apple pie and meat loaf."

The husband took a bite of his supper and asked, "And which one is this?"

Day 147

--- --- --- ---

Chess Enthusiasts

Several chess enthusiasts checked into a hotel and were standing in the lobby, discussing their recent tournament victories. After an hour, the manager came out of the office and asked them to disperse. "But why?" they asked as they moved off.

"Because," the manager explained, "I can't stand chess nuts boastin' in an open foyer."

Day 148

Thankful for Broccoli

A four-year-old boy was asked to pray before dinner. The family members bowed their heads. The boy began his prayer, thanking God for all his friends and family members. Then he began to thank God for the food. He gave thanks for the chicken, the mashed potatoes, the fruit salad, and even the milk. Then he paused, and everyone waited.

After a long silence, the little boy opened one eye, looked at his mother, and whispered, "If I thank God for the broccoli, won't He know that I'm lying?"

Day 149

Preschool Burglar

Three fathers talked about what they would do if a burglar broke into their houses at night.

"I'd call the police," said the first.

"I'd have my wife call the police while I grabbed the baseball bat," growled the second.

The third man, the father of three preschoolers, admitted, "If a burglar came into my room at night, I'd probably get up and take him to the bathroom."

Day 150

Bird Flu

Steve: "How did your parakeet die?"

Fred: "Flu."

Steve: "Don't be silly. Parakeets
don't die from the flu."

Fred: "Mine did. He flew under a bus."

Day 151

- - - - - - -

Wedding Colors

Attending a wedding for the first time,
a little girl whispered to her mother,
"Why is the bride dressed in white?"

"Because white is the color of happiness,"
her mother explained, "and today is the
happiest day in her life."

The child thought for a moment and
then asked, "So why is the groom
wearing black?"

Day 152

- - - - - - -

Sprained Wrist

The doctor was trying to cheer Artie,
who'd sprained his wrist.
"When you get out of this sling,"
the doctor told him, "you'll feel better
than ever. You'll be able to write, catch
Frisbees, and bounce basketballs with
the best of them."

Artie stopped crying and brightened
up. "Wow!" he said. "I've never been
able to bounce a basketball before!"

Day 153

Three-by-Fours

A policeman watched suspiciously as a man stepped out of a van, holding his hands about two feet apart. The man hurried down the street. At the entrance to a building-supply store, the suspect—hands still apart—waited until a customer came through the door. He darted through the open door seemingly afraid to touch the door.

The officer quietly entered the store behind him, just in time to hear the suspect tell a clerk, "I need half a dozen three-by-fours cut exactly this long."

Day 154

Judge and Defendant

Judge: "The last time I saw you, I told you I didn't want to ever see you again."

Defendant: "I told that to the policeman, but he didn't believe me."

Day 155

God's Name

A "pillar of the church" passed away and was on his way to heaven. When he got to the pearly gates, he met an angel. The angel asked him what God's name was. "Oh, that's easy," the man replied. "His name is Andy."

"What makes you think His name is Andy?" the angel asked.

"Well, you see, at church we used to sing this song: 'Andy walks with me, Andy talks with me.'"

Day 156

Top Seven Church Oxymorons

1. Brief meeting

2. Pastor's day off

3. Early sign-up

4. Clear calendar

5. Volunteer waiting list

6. Realistic budget

7. Concluding remarks

Day 157

- - - - - - -

Agnostics

At the close of the service, a visiting preacher remarked to the minister that he thought the singing was terribly poor and asked what the problem was.

The home-team minister replied, "Yes, unfortunately the agnostics here are dreadful."

Day 158

Life of an Octopus

First octopus: "What do you like least about being an octopus?"

Second octopus: "Washing my hands before dinner."

Day 159

---

*You Might Be a
Cross-Country Runner If...*

Your shoes have more miles
on them than your car does.

You need a magnifying glass
to see your name in the paper.

You run farther in a week
than your bus travels for meets.

You can eat your weight in spaghetti.

You schedule dates around meets.

Gatorade is your drug of choice.

Day 160

The Last Day

Gabe: "Why are you down?"

Mike: "My sister said she wouldn't talk to me for two weeks."

Gabe: "Why should that upset you?"

Mike: "Today's the last day."

Day 161

The Best Part of Waking Up

One morning a little boy proudly made coffee for his grandmother.

The grandmother had never in her life had such a bad cup of coffee, and as she forced down the last sip, she noticed three of those little green army guys in the bottom of the cup. She asked, "Honey, why would three little green army guys be in the bottom of my cup?"

Her grandson replied, "You know, Grammy, it's just like on television. 'The best part of waking up is soldiers in your cup.'"

Day 162

Concerned Grandpa

Two neighbors chatting by the fence
noticed a third neighbor pacing
up and down his driveway,
a worried look on his face.

"What's the matter with Ed?"
one asked.

"He's worried about his son,"
the other answered.

"Why? What's he got?"

"The BMW!"

Day 163

What Would You Do?

Maria: "What would you do if you were being chased by a tractor-trailer truck at seventy miles an hour?"

Karl: "Eighty."

Day 164

Turtle Therapy

Why did the turtle
go to the therapist?

He wanted to come
out of his shell.

Day 165

The First Line

An optometrist examining
an elderly patient asked,
"Can you read the fifth line on the chart?"

"No."

"How about the fourth line?"

"No."

"Hmm. Try the second line."

"I can't read that one, either."

"Surely you can read the first line."

"Truth is, I've never learned to read."

HAHA ◎ HAHA ◎ HAHA ◎ HAHA ◎ HAHA ◎ HA

Day 166

A Police Officer's Hat

A police officer was escorting
a prisoner to jail when the officer's
hat blew off down the sidewalk.
"Would you like me to get that for
you?" asked the prisoner.

"You must think I'm an idiot!"
said the officer. "You just wait here,
and I'll get it."

HAHA ◎ HAHA ◎ HAHA ◎ HAHA ◎ HAHA ◎ HAH

Day 167

Definition of Zero

Teacher: "Define 'absolute zero.'"

Greg: "The lowest grade you
can get on a test."

Day 168

Advice Bill

A lawyer and his doctor friend were
working out at the gym.
"I come here to exercise, but people
are always asking me for advice,"
the doctor complained to the lawyer.
"What do you think I should do?"

"Well," said the lawyer, "the next
time you give advice, send a bill."

A few days later, the doctor opened his
mail and found a bill—from the lawyer.

Day 169

Too Far

Judge: "You have been accused of
hitting a comedian with your car,
then dragging him four blocks."

Driver: "It was only three blocks,
Your Honor."

Judge: "That's still carrying
a joke too far."

Day 170

Church Signs

FREE TRIP TO HEAVEN. DETAILS INSIDE.

TRY OUR SUNDAYS. THEY ARE BETTER
THAN BASKIN-ROBBINS.

PEOPLE ARE LIKE TEA BAGS—YOU HAVE
TO PUT THEM IN HOT WATER BEFORE YOU
KNOW HOW STRONG THEY ARE.

RUNNING LOW ON FAITH?
STOP IN FOR A FILL-UP.

IF YOU CAN'T SLEEP,
DON'T COUNT SHEEP.
TALK TO THE SHEPHERD.

Day 171

Church Service Locations

I don't mind going to a church service
in a drive-in theater. But when they
hold the baptisms in a car wash,
that's going too far.

Day 172

A Hungry Lion

A hungry lion was roaming through the jungle looking for something to eat. He came across two men. One was sitting under a tree reading a book; the other was typing away on his laptop. The lion quickly pounced on the man reading the book and devoured him.

Even the king of the jungle knows that readers digest and writers cramp.

Day 173

What Happened?

Molly left a solid object on the
kitchen counter while she went to play.
When she came back four hours later,
the object had completely vanished.
No one touched it or ate it.
What happened?

Molly left an ice cube on the counter.

Day 174

Genghis Khan

A tourist in the Middle East was having a hard time shaking off a street hawker who wanted to sell him the "genuine skull of Genghis Khan." "You're asking far too much, and I don't have luggage space to carry it home. Besides, it's repulsive—and I don't believe it's authentic."

The street seller reached into his bag and came up with a smaller skull, equally gross. He smiled broadly. "Half price—but infinitely more valuable: skull of the great Khan, age twelve."

Day 175

Definitions

Practical nurse: A nurse who marries a wealthy patient.

Specialist: A doctor who prefers a smaller practice and a larger house.

Psychiatry: One profession in which the customer is always wrong.

Day 176

Multitasking

A police officer saw a lady
driving and knitting at the same time,
so after driving next to her for a while,
he yelled, "Pull over!"

"No!" she called back.
"It's a pair of socks!"

Day 177
- - - - - -
Flight Speed

"Look at that speed!" said one hawk to another as a jet-fighter plane zoomed over their heads.

"Hmph!" snorted the other. "You would fly fast, too, if your tail was on fire!"

Day 178

Steak Inflation

"Inflation is creeping up,"
a young man said to his friend.
"Yesterday I ordered a twenty-five-
dollar steak in a restaurant and told
them to put it on my credit card—
and it fit."

Day 179

More Church Signs

THE BEST VITAMIN FOR A CHRISTIAN IS B1.

SOUL FOOD SERVED HERE.

BEAT THE CHRISTMAS RUSH,
COME TO CHURCH THIS SUNDAY.

DON'T GIVE UP. MOSES WAS
ONCE A BASKET CASE!

TO BELITTLE IS TO BE LITTLE.

SO LIVE THAT NO MATTER WHAT HAPPENS,
IT WOULDN'T HAPPEN
TO A NICER PERSON.

Day 180

First Clothing

Why did Adam get the first fig leaf?

Because he wore the plant
in the family.

Day 181

A teacher asked, "Who was the first brother to fly an airplane at Kitty Hawk, North Carolina? Was it Orville or Wilbur?"

"Orville!" shouted one student.

"Wilbur!" shouted another.

"They're both Wright," said a third.

Day 182

Bumper Stickers

EVACUATE THE ROAD—STUDENT DRIVING.

HUG YOUR KIDS AT HOME
AND BELT THEM IN THE CAR.

TRUST IN GOD—BUT LOCK YOUR CAR.

CAUTION! DRIVER APPLYING MAKEUP.

Day 183

Caution: Low Bridge

Two truck drivers came to a low bridge. The clearance sign said ten feet eight inches. When they got out and measured their truck, they discovered their vehicle was eleven feet.

The first man looked at the other and said, "I can't see any cops around. Let's go for it!"

Day 184

Witness

Prosecutor: "How far away from the scene of the crime were you when you heard the first shot?"

Witness: "About thirty feet."

Prosecutor: "How far away were you when the second shot was fired?"

Witness: "About two hundred yards."

HAHA HAHA HAHA HAHA HAHA

Day 185

What Do You Get?

What would you get if you
crossed a baseball player with a frog?

An outfielder who catches
flies and then eats them.

HAHA HAHA HAHA HAHA HAHA

Day 186

Cheap Kittens

"Have you got any
kittens going cheap?"
asked a customer in a pet shop.

"No, sir," replied the owner.
"All our kittens go, 'Meow.'"

Day 187

Humorous Headlines

Shortage of Brains Hampers Research

Bus Strikes Man, Declines Assistance

Airplane Hits Three Houses, Kills Two

Suspect Wounds Wrong Wife,
Says He's Sorry

Day 188

First-Class Conversation

Two well-heeled ladies flying first-class condescended, after an hour of silent boredom, to strike up a conversation with each other. "I just had a delightful note from my son the surgeon," intoned one. "Do you have children?"

"My only son lives in New York."

"And what does he do?"

"He, too, has chosen to pursue the medical profession."

"Lovely. I suppose he's a GP."

"He's a malpractice lawyer."

Day 189

A Skier's Glossary

Alp: One of a number of ski mountains in Europe. Also a request for help.

Avalanche: An actual peril skiers face. See also: blizzard, death on the slopes, first aid, fracture, frostbite, hypothermia, lift collapse.

Bindings: Automatic mechanisms that protect skiers from serious injuries during a fall by releasing skis from boots, sending the skis skittering across the slope where they can trip two other skiers.

Day 190

- - - - - - - -

Spousal Abuse

A woman shoots her husband.
Then she holds him underwater for
over five minutes. Finally, she hangs him.
But one hour later they both go out
together and enjoy a wonderful dinner.
How is this possible?

The woman was a photographer.
She shot a picture of her husband,
developed it, and hung it up to dry.

Day 191

For the Sick

A little girl was sitting in church with her father when she suddenly felt ill. "Daddy," she whispered, "I have to frow up!" Her father told her to hurry to the restroom. In less than two minutes the child was back. "I didn't have to go too far," she explained.

"There's a box by the front door with a sign that says, FOR THE SICK.

Day 192

Council Swindlers

A newspaper ran a blistering editorial in which it stated, "We believe half the members of city council are swindlers." City Hall and its political supporters flooded the editor's phone line for three days.

Finally, a retraction was published.
It read:
"We now believe half the members of city council are not swindlers."

Day 193

Cut and Spread

What is cut and spread out
on the table but never eaten?

A deck of cards.

Day 194

----- -----

Planet Life

NASA scientists have an ingenious way of determining whether a distant planet is inhabited. They program the landing craft to mechanically dig a hole in the surface.

If no one comes to stand around and watch, they know the planet is void of life.

Day 195

Texas vs. Boston

A Texan was trying to impress a guy from Boston with a graphic account of the heroism at the Alamo. He said, "I guess you don't have many heroes where you come from?"

The man from Boston replied, "Well, sir, have you ever heard of Paul Revere?"

And the Texan replied, "Paul Revere? Isn't he the guy who ran for help?"

Day 196

- - - - - - -

Kindergarten Questions

A group of kindergarteners was on a class outing to its local police station where the kids saw pictures, tacked to a bulletin board of the ten most wanted men. One of the youngsters pointed to a picture and asked if it really was the photo of a wanted person. "Yes," answered the policeman.

"Well," wondered the child, "why didn't you keep him when you took his picture?"

Day 197

--- --- --- --- --- ---

Acts 2:38

Sister Deena had just returned home
when she was startled by a burglar.
With great biblical authority she yelled,
"Stop! Acts 2:38!" which says to "turn
from your sin." The thief stopped dead
in his tracks. Then the woman calmly
called the police.

As the officer cuffed the man,
he asked the burglar, "Why did you
stop your burgling? All the old lady did
was yell a Bible verse at you."

"Bible verse?" replied the crook.
"She said she had an ax and two .38s!"

Day 198

Learning the Presidents

Teacher: "Zach, you need to work on learning the presidents. When I was your age, I could name all of them."

Zach: "Yes, but then there were only four or five."

Day 199

Homework Excuses

"I left it in my shirt, and my mother put it into the washing machine."

"My sister used it to line the rabbit's cage."

"A sudden gust of wind blew it out of my hand, and I never saw it again."

"My friend fell into a lake, and I jumped in to rescue him. My homework didn't make it, though."

"Our furnace stopped working, and we had to burn it to keep ourselves from freezing."

"I didn't do it because I didn't want the other kids in the class to look bad."

Day 200

Fishing Librarians

How do librarians catch fish?

With bookworms.

Day 201

Knock-Knock, Aileen

Knock-knock.

Who's there?

Aileen.

Aileen who?

Aileen piece of meat
is good for the waistline.

Day 202

Knock-Knock, Dewey

Knock-knock.

Who's there?

Dewey.

Dewey who?

Dewey have to keep telling these dumb jokes?

Day 203

Egyptian Bone Specialist

What do you call a bone
specialist from Egypt?

A Cairopractor.

Day 204

An Experienced Glazier

The manager of a glass and window
company advertised in the paper
for experienced glaziers. Since
a good glass man is hard to find,
he was pleased when a man who
called about he job said he
had twelve years of experience.
"Where have you worked as a glazier?"
the manager asked.

The man replied, "Krispy Kreme."

Day 205

Democrat or Republican?

It was local election time, and the
candidate was visiting all the houses
in his area. At one house,
a small boy answered the door.

"Tell me, young man," said the politician,
"is your mommy in the Republican
Party or the Democratic Party?"

"Neither," said the child.
"She's in the bathroom."

Day 206

Political Definitions

Monologue: A conversation between a politician and somebody else.

Diplomacy: The art of letting someone else have your own way.

Minority rule: A newborn baby just home from the hospital.

Day 207

One-Dollar Bills

A politician asked a minister,
"What is something the government
can do to help the church?"

"Well," the minister replied,
"quit making one-dollar bills."

Day 208

Army Hours

Army doctor: "You're looking pale, Corporal. When did you eat last?"

Corporal: "Nineteen fifty-nine, sir."

Army doctor: "What? How could you survive so long?"

Corporal: "Well, sir, it's only 2130 now."

Day 209

Rough Commute

Why was the computer so tired when
it got home from the office?

Because it had a hard drive.

Day 210

Short Sermons

A minister preached a very short sermon. He explained, "My dog got into my study and chewed up some of my notes."

At the close of the service a visitor asked, "If your dog ever has pups, please let my pastor have one of them."

Day 211

A Canine Complex

A man walked into the office of a psychiatrist and sat down to explain his problem. "Doctor, I have this problem," the man said. "I keep hallucinating that I'm a dog. It's crazy. I don't know what to do!"

"A common canine complex," said the doctor reassuringly. "Relax. Come here and lie down on the couch."

"Oh, I can't, doctor," the man said nervously. "I'm not allowed on the furniture."

Day 212

------- -------

What Am I?

I can sizzle like bacon, and I am made
with an egg. I have plenty of backbone,
but lack a good leg. I peel layers like an
onion, but still remain whole. I can be
long, like a flagpole; yet fit in a hole.
What am I?

A snake.

Day 213

Family Laziness

"When Abraham Lincoln was your age," a man said to his lazy teenage son, "he was chopping wood, plowing, and hunting for food."

"When he was your age," the boy responded, "he was president of the United States."

Day 214

-- -- -- -- -- --

Happiness

A rich man and a poor man were arguing about which was happiest. "My millions make me extremely happy," said the rich man. "All you have to show are six children and a lot of debt."

"But I'm more contented than you," countered the poor man. "If I had your money, I'd want more. If you had six children, you wouldn't want any more."

Day 215

Fishermen and Hypochondriacs

Hilda: "What do fishermen and hypochondriacs have in common?"

Joe: "They don't really have to catch anything to be happy."

Day 216

You Might Be a College Student If...

You have ever price-shopped
for Top Ramen.

You have ever written a check
for forty-five cents.

You celebrate when you find a quarter.

You have ever seen two consecutive
sunrises without sleeping.

You can pack your worldly possessions
into the back of a pickup (in one trip).

You are personally keeping the local
pizza place from bankruptcy.

Day 217

Definitions

Computer Programmer:
A happy-go-lucky human trained to
consume seven pizzas a week and
interrupt normal conversations to
consult aloud with imaginary colleagues.

Electrician: Someone who's always
wiring for more money.

Historian: Someone who just
can't let the past lie.

Mountain climber: An athlete
with the gift of grab.

Nuclear scientist: A professional
with a lot of ions in the fire.

Day 218

The Secret to Happiness

Why are frogs
so happy?

They eat whatever
bugs them.

Day 219

Benefits of Being 103

A reporter interviewed a 103-year-old woman: "And what is the best thing about being 103?" the reporter asked.

The woman simply replied, "No peer pressure."

Day 220

Swimming

If swimming is so good
for your figure,
how do you explain whales?

HAHA ◎ HAHA ◎ HAHA ◎ HAHA ◎ HAHA

Day 221

- - - - - - -

What Am I?

The beginning of eternity;
The end of time and space.
The beginning of every end,
And the end of every place.
What am I?

The letter *E.*

HAHA ◎ HAHA ◎ HAHA ◎ HAHA ◎ HAHA

Day 222

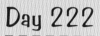

Dr. Smith and Dr. Jones

Maggie woke up one day with
a toothache and went to the only
dental practice in town to have it fixed.
The dental practice had two partners,
Dr. Smith and Dr. Jones.

Dr. Smith has a beautiful smile,
while Dr. Jones has a mouth of ugly,
crooked teeth. Who should Maggie
see about the toothache?

Dr. Jones. Since it is the only dental
practice in town, Dr. Jones must fix
Dr. Smith's teeth and vice versa.

Day 223

Diet Rules

If you eat something and no one sees you eat it, it has no calories.

If you drink a diet soda with a candy bar, the calories in the candy bar are canceled out by the diet soda.

When you eat with someone, the calories don't count if you don't eat more than he or she does.

Foods such as hot chocolate, pancakes, and Sara Lee cheesecake used for medicinal purposes never count.

If you fatten up everyone else around you, then you look thinner.

Day 224

A linguistics professor was lecturing his class one day. "In the English language," he said, "a double negative forms a positive. In other languages, such as Russian, a double negative is still a negative. However, there is no language wherein a double positive can form a negative."

A voice from the back of the room said, "Yeah, right."

Day 225

Knock-Knock, Honey

Knock-knock.

Who's there?

Honey hive.

Honey hive who?

Honey, hive got a crush on you.

Day 226

------- -------

The Ark

As Noah and his family were
disembarking from the ark,
they paused on a ridge to look back.
"We should have done something,
Noah," his wife said. "That old hulk of
an ark will sit there and be an eyesore
on the landscape for years to come."

"Everything's taken care of,"
Noah assured her. "I left the two
termites aboard."

Day 227

*You Might Be a Missionary or
Missionary's Kid If. . .*

You don't think two hours
is a long sermon.

You refer to gravel roads as highways.

Fitting fifteen or more people
into a car seems normal.

You realize that furlough
is not a vacation.

You do your devotions
in another language.

Day 228

Tiger at the Zoo

A police officer saw a woman sitting in her car with a tiger in the front seat next to her. The officer said, "It's against the law to have that tiger in your car. Take him to the zoo."

The next day the police officer saw the same woman in the same car with the same tiger. He said, "I told you yesterday to take that tiger to the zoo!"

The woman replied, "I did. He had such a good time, today we're going to the beach!"

Day 229

What Am I?

Lovely and round,
I shine with pale light,
Grown in the darkness,
A lady's delight.
What am I?

A pearl.

Day 230

-- -- -- -- -- --

*You May Be Obsessing over
Your Computer If…*

You turn off your computer and get
an awful empty feeling, as if you just
pulled the plug on a loved one.

You start using smileys :-)
in your snail mail.

You find yourself typing "com"
after every period when using
a word processor.com.

In real-life conversations, you don't
laugh, you just say, "LOL, LOL."

Day 231

Bathroom Scales

A certain bathroom-scale manufacturer was very proud of the new model being introduced at the trade fair: "It's calibrated to one one-hundredth of a pound; it can measure your height in feet or meters; it gives you a readout via an LED or human voice simulator; and that's not all. . . ."

"Very impressive," interrupted a not-too-slender home furnishings sales rep, "but before I place an order I'll have to try it out." No sooner had the sales rep stepped on the scale than a loud, very human-sounding voice issued forth: "One at a time, please, one at a time."

Day 232

Mrs. Ferguson's Indigestion

The old family physician took his son into partnership after the young man received his medical degree. The old doctor then went off on a two-week vacation. When he got home, he asked his son if there'd been any problems at the clinic. The son said no, everything went well. "In fact," he said, "you know that rich old widow, Mrs. Ferguson? I cured her of her chronic indigestion."

"Well, that's fine," said the old doctor. "But Mrs. Ferguson's indigestion is what put you through medical school."

Day 233

The Top Five Signs You're a Lousy Cook

1. Your family automatically heads for the table every time they hear the smoke alarm.

2. Your kids know what "peas porridge in the pot nine days old" tastes like.

3. Your kids' favorite smoothie is Pepto-Bismol.

4. No matter what you do, the gravy still turns bright purple.

5. You burned the house down trying to make freezer jam.

Day 234

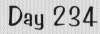

Answers to Fifth-Grade Science Exams

H2O is hot water,
and CO2 is cold water.

Nitrogen is not found in Ireland
because it is not found in a free state.

To collect fumes of sulfur, hold a
deacon over a flame in a test tube.

A fossil is an extinct animal.
The older it is, the more extinct it is.

When you smell an odorless gas,
it is probably carbon monoxide.

Three kinds of blood vessels are
arteries, veins, and caterpillars.

Day 235

A Pampered Cow

What do you get
from a pampered cow?

Spoiled milk.

Day 236

Broken Engagement

Donald: "I hear you broke off your engagement. What happened?"

Daisy: "Oh, it's just that my feelings for him have changed."

Donald: "Are you returning the ring?"

Daisy: "Oh no. My feelings for the ring haven't changed."

Day 237

What Men Really Mean

"Take a break, honey, you're
working too hard" really means:
"I can't hear the game over the
vacuum cleaner."

"Can I help you with dinner?" really means:
"Why isn't it on the table yet?"

"I missed you" really means
"My socks need washing, and
we're out of toilet paper."

Day 238

The Telephone Pole

Some people were marveling at the scene of an accident where one of them miraculously had walked away from the mishap without a scratch the night before. "Wow, that was some smashup," said one.

"Totaled the car," said another.

"How'd it happen?" asked a third.

The victim pointed to a tilted telephone pole. "See that?"

"Yeah."

"I didn't."

Day 239

-- -- -- -- --

What do you call. . . ?

What do you call a watch
worn on a belt?

A waist of time.

Day 240

Dinner Party

A couple was enjoying a dinner party at the home of friends. Near the end of the meal, the wife slapped her husband's arm.

"That's the third time you've gone for dessert," she said. "The hostess must think you're an absolute pig."

"I doubt that," the husband said. "I've been telling her it's for you."

Day 241

Veterinarian and Policeman

In a small town the veterinarian, who was also the chief of police, was awakened by the telephone.

"Please hurry!" said the woman's voice on the other end of the line.

"Do you need the police or a vet?" he asked.

"Both," the woman replied. "I'm not able to get my dog's mouth open, and there's a burglar's leg in it."

Day 242

Driver's License

A cop pulls a woman over and says, "Let me see your driver's license, lady."

The woman replies, "I wish you people would get your act together. One day you take away my license and the next day you ask me to show it."

Day 243

Pizza Tips

"What is the usual tip?" Mr. Wilson asked the pizza delivery boy.

"Well," the boy replied, "this is my first trip here, but the other guys say if I get a quarter out of you, I'll be doing great."

"Is that so?" snorted Mr. Wilson. "Well, just to show them how wrong they are, I'll give you five dollars."

"Thanks!" replied the delivery guy. "I'll put this toward my textbooks."

"What are you studying?" asked Mr. Wilson.

The young man smiled and said, "Psychology."

Day 244

A Young Businessman

A young businessman had just started his own firm. He rented a beautiful office and had it furnished with the very best. Sitting at his fancy desk, he saw a man come into the outer office. Wishing to appear busy to his potential first customer, he picked up the telephone and improvised a one-sided conversation with a big spender.

He threw big figures around and made giant commitments. Finally he hung up and asked the visitor, "May I help you?"

The man answered, "Sure. I've come to install that phone!"

Day 245

Sunday School Lessons

A father was teaching his son
to admire the beauty in nature.
"Look, Will," he exclaimed, "isn't that
a beautiful sunset that God painted?"

"It sure is, Dad," the son agreed,
"especially since God had to paint it
with His left hand."

The father was bewildered. "What do
you mean—His left hand?"

"Well," he said, "my Sunday school
teacher said that Jesus is sitting on
God's right hand."

Day 246

- - - - - - - -

Sun's Greetings

What did the sun say when
it was introduced to the earth?

"Pleased to heat you."

Day 247

- - - - - - -

A Robber in the House

The wife of a U.S. Representative
shook him awake one night.

"Jim, there's a robber in the house,"
she whispered. "Get up."

The representative mumbled in reply,
"No, dear. In the Senate, yes.
But not in the House."

Day 248

Family Politics

A campaigning Democrat was interrupted time after time by a man in the back of the crowd who kept proclaiming loudly that he was a Republican.

"And why are you a Republican?" the politician finally asked.

"My father was a Republican and his father before him!" the man yelled.

"Well, suppose your father and grandfather were fools. What would that make you?"

"A Democrat!"

Day 249

Ocean Cleaner

What kind of animal
cleans the ocean?

A mermaid!

Day 250

- - - - - - -

Knock-Knock, Deluxe

Knock-knock.

Who's there?

Deluxe.

Deluxe who?

Deluxe Ness Monster.

Day 251

The Over-Forty Basketball League

I play in the over-forty basketball
league. We don't have jump balls.
The ref just puts the ball on the floor,
and whoever can bend over and
pick it up gets possession.

Day 252

P.E. Class Excuses

"My son Peter is under doctor's care and should not take P.E. today. Please execute him."

"Please excuse Melody from class yesterday. She was sick and I had her shot."

"Dear Coach: Please excuse John from suiting-up on January 28, 29, 30, 31, 32, and also 33."

"Please excuse Roland from P.E. for a few days. Yesterday he fell out of a tree and misplaced his hip."

"John has not been in class because he had two teeth taken out of his face."

Day 253

What Am I?

I am used to bat with,
yet I never get a hit.
I am near a ball,
yet it is never thrown.
What am I?

Eyelashes.

Day 254

What Am I?

I can be cool,
but I am never cold.
I can be sorry,
but I won't be guilty.
I can be spooked,
but I can't be anxious.
I can be sweet,
but I don't include candy.
I can be swallowed,
but I will never be eaten.
What am I?

Words with double letters.

Day 255

Prayer Request

A nearsighted minister glanced
at the note that Mrs. Edwards had
sent to him by an usher.

The note read: "Phil Edwards having
gone to sea, his wife desires the prayers
of the congregation for his safety."

The minister failed to observe the
punctuation, however, and surprised
the congregation when he read aloud,
"Phil Edwards, having gone to sea
his wife, desires the prayers of the
congregation for his safety."

Day 256

Free Train Ride

A con artist was trying to finesse a free train ride. When the conductor came down the aisle, the man pointed to his dog with a gesture of helpless agitation. "He ate my ticket!"

The conductor frowned. "Then I strongly suggest you buy him dessert."

Day 257

Free Financing

Salesman: "You make a small down payment, but then you don't make any payments for six months."

Customer: "Who told you about me?"

Day 258

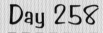

Gender Punctuation

An English professor wrote the
following words on the blackboard:
"Woman without her man is nothing."
He then requested that his students
punctuate it correctly.

The men wrote:
"Woman, without her man, is nothing."

The women wrote:
"Woman! Without her, man is nothing."

Day 259

That's Show Business

Dan: "I just finished a long
run on Broadway."

Zach: "What play were you in?"

Dan: "Oh, I wasn't in any play.
A mugger chased me for ten blocks."

Day 260

Turkey Day

The pro football team had just finished its daily practice when a large turkey came strutting onto the field. The turkey walked up to the head coach and demanded a tryout. Everyone stared in silence as the turkey caught pass after pass and ran through the defensive line.

The coach shouted, "You're terrific! Sign up for the season, and I'll see to it that you get a huge signing bonus."

"Forget the bonus," the turkey said. "All I want to know is, does the season go past Thanksgiving Day?"

Day 261

- - - - - - - -

Question

What question can
you never answer with a yes?

"Are you sleeping?"

Day 262

Rock Group

What rock group has four members,
all of whom are dead,
one of whom was assassinated?

Mount Rushmore.

Day 263

- - - - - - - -

What Am I?

A teacher had just discussed magnets
with her class. A bit later, she said,
"My name begins with M,
and I pick things up.
What am I?"

Niles thought for a moment
and answered, "Mom!"

Day 264

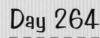

A Frustrated Father

A frustrated father vented,
"When I was a teenager and got
in trouble, I was sent to my room
without supper. But my son has
his own television, telephone,
computer, and CD player in his room."

"So what do you do to him?"
asked his friend.

"I send him to my room!"
exclaimed the father.

Day 265

The Top Five Reasons We Are Overweight

1. Hey, we get eighty channels of great television twenty-four hours a day. There's no time to exercise.

2. Girl Scout cookies get better every year.

3. The colossal failure of the Salad King drive-thru franchise.

4. Just to spite Richard Simmons.

5. Addition of a diet soda does NOT mean your bacon cheeseburger/chili fries combo is a healthy meal.

Day 266

History Lesson

Teacher: "Why are you reading the last pages of your history book first?"

Student: "I want to know how it ends."

Day 267

Bills and Report Cards

A mother and father were
paying bills one evening.
"Groceries, gasoline, electricity—
everything is going up,"
mused the father.

"I know," agreed the mother.
"Nothing ever goes down."

"Well, look at this!"
exclaimed their son, walking into the
room with his report card.

Day 268

Hemingway Hall

A man was visiting a college. He paused to admire the new Hemingway Hall that had recently been constructed on campus. "It's marvelous to see a building named for Ernest Hemingway," he said.

"Actually," said the guide, "it's named for William Hemingway. No relation."

The visitor was astonished. "Was William Hemingway a writer, too?" he asked.

"Oh yes," said his guide. "He wrote the check."

Day 269

The Parson's Wife

The poor country parson was livid when he confronted his wife with the receipt for a 250-dollar dress she had bought.

"How could you do this?" he exclaimed.

"I don't know," she wailed. It was like the devil was whispering to me, 'Wow, you look great in that dress. You should buy it.'"

The husband persisted, "Just tell him, 'Get behind me, Satan!'"

"I did," replied his wife, "but then he said, 'It looks great from back there, too!'"

Day 270

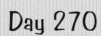

Cleaning Up the Mess

A parsonage son said to his mother, "I've decided that I want to be a preacher so that I can clean up the mess the world is in."

"That's just wonderful," purred his mother. "You can go upstairs and start with your room."

Day 271

Nine-Dollar Sundae

A reindeer walked into an ice cream shop, hopped up on a stool at the counter, and ordered a one-dollar hot butterscotch sundae. When it arrived, he put a ten-dollar bill on the counter. But the waiter thought he wouldn't know anything about money and gave him only a dollar in change.

"You know," said the waiter, "we don't get many reindeer in here. In fact, I think you're the first one we've ever had."

"Well," the reindeer replied, "at nine dollars a sundae you probably won't get many more."

Day 272

------- -------

Half-Time Speech

A well-known college football coach
has been heard admitting,
"I give the same half-time speech over
and over. It works best when
my players are better than
the other coach's players."

Day 273

Drought Baptisms

A drought in Georgia began to affect how the churches in many communities had to conduct baptisms.

The Baptists took up sprinkling, the Methodists used damp cloths, and the Presbyterians gave out rain checks.

HAHA ◎ HAHA ◎ HAHA ◎ HAHA ◎ HAHA ◎ HA

Day 274

OJ Skills

Why was the employee
fired from the orange juice factory?

He couldn't concentrate.

HAHA ◎ HAHA ◎ HAHA ◎ HAHA ◎ HAHA ◎ HA

Day 275

Maine to Florida

What goes from Maine
to Florida without moving?

The highway.

Day 276

Four-Way Stop

Four cars come to a four-way stop, each coming from either north, south, east, or west. It isn't clear who arrived first, so they all go at the same time. No one crashes, but all four cars successfully continue on their way. How is this possible?

They all made right-hand turns.

Day 277

Like Father, Like Son

A woman was admiring
her friend's newborn son.
"He certainly favors his father," she said.

"You're right about that. Sleeps
all the time, doesn't say anything,
and doesn't have any hair."

Day 278

Medical School

A bright farm boy announced
to his weathered old dad,
"I've decided to go to medical school
and study anesthesiology."

"I wouldn't, if I were you, boy,"
the father said. "By the time you
graduate, they'll have a cure for it."

Day 279

Snip Snip

Two barbershops
were in red-hot competition.
One put up a sign advertising
haircuts for seven dollars.

His competitor put
up one that read,
WE REPAIR SEVEN-DOLLAR HAIRCUTS.

Day 280

Police Academy 101

During a police academy class, the instructor began, "If you were called to an automobile accident with the chief of police in one car and the mayor in the other car…and then you looked down the street and saw several fire trucks were desperately fighting a fire in the courthouse…what would you do under these circumstances?"

One of the new recruits answered, "I'd remove my uniform and mingle with the crowd."

Day 281

A Bad Driver

"My dad must be a pretty
bad driver," said Brad.

"What do you mean?" asked Bret.

"I was with him when he got pulled
over for speeding yesterday. The officer
recognized him and wrote him
out a season ticket."

Day 282

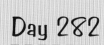

Marriage

In the first year of marriage,
the man speaks and the woman listens.

In the second year, the woman speaks
and the man listens.

In the third year, they both speak
and the neighbors listen.

Day 283

Quick Quips on Marriage

"A husband is someone who takes out the trash and gives the impression that he just cleaned the whole house."

"My wife keeps complaining I never listen to her—or something like that."

"Love is what happens when imagination overpowers common sense."

"Keep your eyes wide open before marriage—and half-shut afterward."

"Marriage is like a violin— after the music stops, the strings are still attached."

Day 284

The Lovesick Bull

What did the lovesick bull
say to the cow?

"When I fall in love,
it will be for heifer."

Day 285

Knock-Knock, Willoughby

Knock-knock.

Who's there?

Willoughby.

Willoughby who?

Willoughby my Valentine?

Day 286

Ten Commandments

A little boy in Sunday school was asked what commandment he would break if he stayed home from Sunday school. He replied, "The fourth one: 'Keep the Sabbath Day holy.'"

Then he was asked what commandment he would break if he pulled his dog's tail. He hesitated then said, "I don't know the number, but it goes like this: 'What God has joined together, let no man pull apart.'"

Day 287

Lights on the Ark

What kind of lights did Noah
have on the ark?

Floodlights.

Day 288

First Wedding

A just-out-of-seminary pastor was about to conduct his first wedding and was worried sick. An elderly preacher gave him some advice: "If you lose your place in the ceremony book or you forget your lines, start quoting scriptures until you find your place."

The wedding day came. And sure enough, the young man forgot where he was in the ritual. Unfortunately, the only verse he could think of was, "Father, forgive them, for they know not what they do."

Day 289

An Exotic Bird

An affluent man paid twenty-five
thousand dollars for
an exotic bird for his mother.
"How did you like the bird?"
he asked her later.

She responded, "It was delicious."

Day 290

Italian Vacation

A man vacationing in Italy happened to be in the bathroom of his hotel suite when a devastating earthquake shook the building to its frame. Pictures dropped from the walls. Plaster fell from the ceilings. Screams from adjoining rooms and sirens from the streets below filled the air. Members of the hotel staff hurried from room to room to check on their guests.

When they arrived at the American's suite, they found him cowering by the toilet. "I swear," he cried, shaking his head in disbelief, "all I did was pull the chain!"

Day 291

─ ─ ─ ─ ─ ─ ─

Heaven and Earth

Toward the end of a particularly
trying round of golf, Troy was the
picture of frustration. He'd hit too
many fat shots. Finally he blurted
out to his caddie, "I'd move heaven and
earth to break a hundred
on this course."

"Try heaven," replied the caddie.
"You've already moved most
of the earth."

Day 292

Practical Camping Tips

When using a public campground,
a tuba placed on your picnic table
will keep the sites on either
side of you vacant.

When smoking fish, never inhale.

You'll never be lost if you remember
that moss always grows on the north
side of your compass.

You can duplicate the warmth of a
down-filled sleeping bag by climbing
into a plastic garbage bag
with several geese.

Day 293

What Am I?

When full, I can point the way,
but when empty, nothing moves me.
I have two skins—one outside
and one inside.
What am I?

A glove.

Day 294

Tenth Grade

A tenth-grade boy came home
with a poor report card. As he handed
it to his father, he asked,

"What do you think is wrong, Dad,
my heredity or my environment?"

Day 295

A Bundle of Joy

Pastor George and wife, Sally, brought their new bundle of joy home to the parsonage. Days went by with Sally watching every move baby Georgie made while George Sr. busied himself with theological thoughts. Naturally the care began to take its toll on Sally, causing her husband to gallantly announce: "I know you're having a lot of trouble with Georgie, dear, but keep in mind, 'the hand that rocks the cradle is the hand that rules the world.'"

Sally replied, "How about taking over the world for a few hours while I go shopping?"

Day 296

Honeymoon Over?

"I heard you and your wife arguing last night," a man remarked to his newly married neighbor. "Honeymoon over?"

"Not really. It's just that when it comes to some things, I won't change my opinion and she won't change the subject."

Day 297

------- ------- ------- ------- ------- ------- -------

The First Computer

What kind of computer would
you find in the Garden of Eden?

Adam's Apple.

Day 298

- - - - - -

What Am I?

I am strongest when you
view me whole, but I am often
found in other shapes. I move the
oceans with my incredible strength,
and an explorer with a name like
"powerful bicep" was the first
to walk on me.
What am I?

The moon.

Day 299

--- --- --- --- --- ---

The Nearest Railroad

A stranger frantically ran up to a farmer's house, pounded his fist on the door, and demanded, "Where's the nearest railroad station, and what time's the next train to the city?"

The farmer came to the screen door and thought a moment. "Cut through my back hayfield, and you ought to reach the crossroads station in time for the 5:40. Actually, if my bull spots you, I expect you'll make the 5:15."

Day 300

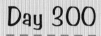

Saving Lives

A professor was discussing a particularly complicated concept. A premed student rudely interrupted him and asked, "Why do we have to learn this pointless information?"

"To save lives," the professor responded quickly and continued the lecture.

A few minutes later, the same student spoke up again. "So how does physics save lives?" he inquired.

"It keeps people like you out of medical school," replied the professor.

Day 301

Checkup

A man came home from
the doctor's office, and his wife
asked how he had checked out.

"Hmph," the man said disgustedly.
"He told me I'm either forty pounds
too heavy or four inches too short."

Day 302

Baby Draft

Why did the army begin
drafting babies?

It was trying to
build up the infantry.

Day 303

The Patient Waiter

A customer was continually bothering the waiter in a restaurant. First, he asked that the air-conditioning be turned up because he was too hot; then he asked that it be turned down because he was too cold.

That continued for about half an hour. The waiter was very patient, walking back and forth and never once getting angry. Finally, a second customer asked why they just didn't ask the man to leave.

"Oh, I don't mind," said the waiter calmly. "We don't even have an air conditioner."

Day 304

- - - - - -

Doggie Bag

While eating in an expensive restaurant, a patron overheard the gentleman at the next table ask the waitress to pack the leftovers for their dog.

The gentleman's young son then exclaimed, "Whoopee! We're going to get a dog!"

Day 305

Teacher Questions

Teacher: "If you have fifteen potatoes and must divide them equally among five people, how would you do it?"

Shelly: "I'd mash them."

Day 306

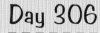

Sunday School Proverbs

The children's Sunday school department was undertaking a study of the book of Proverbs. To illustrate what proverbs are, Miss Daisy collected the first phrase of a bunch of traditional ones and asked the children to creatively complete them. Here are some results:

Better to be safe than...
punch a fifth grader.

Strike while the...bug is close.

Don't bite the hand that...looks dirty.

The pen is mightier than the...pigs.

Day 307

Eating the Apple

"When did Adam and Eve eat the apple?" a Sunday school teacher asked.

"In the summertime," answered a student.

"Why, Brenda, how do you know that?" the teacher asked.

"Well, we all know it was just before the fall."

Day 308

Big Cat

Which big cat should you never
play a board game with?

A cheetah.

Day 309

- - - - - - -

Proofreading

A news-editing professor, grading
the results of a proofreading test,
was devastated to notice this
sentence in his own instructions:

"Read slowly and carefully
o sure nothing missing."

Day 310

Chickens

The customer wanted to buy a chicken and the butcher had only one in stock. He weighed it and said, "This one's a beauty. That will be $4.25."

"Oh, but that isn't quite large enough," said the customer. The butcher put the chicken back in the refrigerator, rolled it around on the ice several times, then placed it back on the scale again. "This one is $5.50," he said, adding his thumb to the weight.

"Oh, that's great!" said the customer. "I'll take both of them, please."

Day 311

How to Annoy Your Man
on Super Bowl Sunday

Take the batteries out
of all the remote controls.

Show a sudden interest in every aspect
of the game. Especially have him define
the offside rule several times.

Plug in a boom box and do
your Dancerobics routine.

Invite your mother over for the game.

Day 312

Canoeing

"I thought I told you to keep
an eye on your cousin!"
the mother impatiently barked.
"Where is he?"

"Well," her son replied thoughtfully,
"if he knows as much about canoeing
as he thinks he does, he's out canoeing.
If he knows as little as I think he does,
he's out swimming."

Day 313

Tennis Lessons

Ella: "I just adore tennis.
I could play like this forever."

Mark: "You will, if you don't
take lessons."

Day 314

Tractor Puzzle

You move to an island in the middle of a lake. There has never been a bridge connecting the island to the mainland. Every day a tractor and wagon gives rides around the island to tourists. Puzzled as to how the tractor had gotten onto the island, you ask around. You find out that the tractor was not built on the island and was not transported to the island by boat or by air. How did the tractor get to the island?

The owner waited until winter and then drove the tractor over on the frozen lake.

Day 315

What Am I?

A wee man in a little red coat.
Staff in his hand,
and stone in his throat.
What am I?

A cherry.

Day 316

What Kind?

What kind of snake
is good at math?

An adder.

Day 317

Counting to Ten

The first-grade teacher
on the opening day of school asked
a student if he knew how to count.

"Yes," he beamed.
"I learned from my daddy."

"Let me hear you count
from five to ten."
The child did as he was asked.

"Now, do you know what
comes after ten?"

"Jack!"

Day 318

Nighttime Prayers

A mother peeked in to hear
her child say his prayers at bedtime.
The boy had been in a fussy mood,
and his sentences came
in mumbled fragments.

"I can't hear what you're saying,"
his mother gently admonished.

"I'm not praying to you,"
the child pouted.

Day 319

- - - - - - - -

Two Birds

"I really appreciate your coming out to our house this late at night," remarked a sick patient.

"No problem," said the doctor. "I had to come see Mr. Oaks just down the road, anyway. This way I can kill two birds with one stone."

Day 320

The Most Important Invention

"What do you think was the most important invention in all of history?" the teacher asked her class.

"The automobile," answered one student.

"The airplane," answered the second.

"The nuclear submarine," answered the third.

"The credit card," answered the fourth.

Day 321

A Youthful Appearance

Three eligible widows were discussing several eligible widowers in their church.

"Now George is a nice man," remarked one, "and he really doesn't look sixty."

Another was far less impressed by George's youthful appearance. "Well," she said, "he used to look sixty."

Day 322

Bad Habit

How did the carpenter
break his teeth?

He chewed on his nails.

Day 323

Grandchildren

Two children were caught in mischief by their grandmother. Happily, she chose not to punish them. "I remember being young once, too," she mused.

"Gee, Grandma," said one of the children, wide eyed. "You sure have an incredible memory!"

Day 324

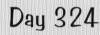

Fisherman's Tale

A fisherman was bragging about
a monster of a fish he caught.
A friend broke in and chided,
"Yeah, I saw a picture of that fish,
and he was all of six inches long."

"Yeah," said the proud fisherman.
"But after battling for three hours,
a fish can lose a lot of weight."

Day 325

Fractions

Teacher: "If I cut a steak in two, then cut the halves in two, what do I get?"

Student: "Quarters."

Teacher: "Very good. And what would I get if I cut it again?"

Student: "Eighths."

Teacher: "Great job! And if I cut it again?"

Student: "Sixteenths."

Teacher: "Wonderful! And again?"

Student: "Hamburger."

Day 326

It's All Fun and Games

Why didn't they play
cards on Noah's ark?

Because Noah sat on the deck.

Day 327

Sermonettes

A clock-watching parishioner couldn't refrain from commenting to the minister after a church service, "Your sermons begin well enough, but why do you make them so long? I'm afraid a lot of folks lose interest."

The minister had a ready reply: "Sermonettes make for Christianettes."

Day 328

Assistant Pastor's Sermon

Pastor: "How did the assistant pastor's sermon go Sunday?"

Church member: "It was a poor sermon. Nothing in it at all."

Upon seeing the assistant pastor:
Pastor: "How did it go Sunday morning?"

Assistant: "Excellently. I didn't have time to prepare anything myself, so I preached one of your sermons."

Day 329

Apple or Cookie?

At a church dinner, there was
a pile of apples on one end
of a table with a sign that read,
TAKE ONLY ONE APPLE,
PLEASE. GOD IS WATCHING.

On the other end of the table
was a pile of cookies where
a youth had placed a sign saying,
TAKE ALL THE COOKIES YOU WANT.
GOD IS WATCHING THE APPLES.

Day 330

The Latest Government Study

Did you hear about the latest
government study on aging?

It cost 240 million dollars
and provided compelling evidence
that the average American
is growing older.

Day 331

Humorous Headlines

Rash of Accidents Keeps
EMT Crews Hopping

Dinner Theater Relies
on Seasoned Cast

Slain Youth Found Alive

Cars Collide; One Charged
with Abusive Language

Day 332

Golfing Improvement

Golfer: "Notice any improvement since last year?"

Caddy: "Polished your clubs, didn't you?"

Day 333

What Are They?

At night they come
without being called
And move around without
being walled.
But at the very first sign of light,
They disappear back into the night.
What are they?

Stars.

Day 334

Young Mother

At 3:00 in the morning, a young wife shook her husband awake. "What is it?" he asked groggily. "The baby," she reminded him.

The husband sat up and listened a full minute. "But I don't hear her crying," he protested.

"I know. It's your turn to go see why not."

Day 335

Child-Rearing Tips

Two mothers were comparing child-rearing notes. "I just can't seem to get my children's attention," said one. "They stay mesmerized in front of the television set. I say things to them and call for them, and they're oblivious to every word."

"Try sitting in an easy chair and looking like you're relaxed," said the other. "That gets my children's attention without fail."

Day 336

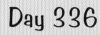

Retirement Age

The firm's administrator really was taken by the character of the job applicant, but she strongly suspected the woman was past retirement age.

"On your application,"
the administrator remarked tactfully,
"I see your birthday is the same
as my mother's: September 6.
May I ask what year?"

"Every year," came the stoic reply.

Day 337

Wandering Numbers

What numbers are always
wandering around?

Roamin' numerals.

Day 338

Three Wise Women

You do know what would have happened if it had been three wise women instead of men, don't you?

They would have asked for directions, arrived on time, helped deliver the baby, cleaned the stable, made a casserole, and brought disposable diapers as a gift!

Day 339

Bloopers

"If across-the-board salary raises are not approved for District Five teachers, several have threatened to abandon their pests."

"Mrs. Jones will sink two numbers. She will be accompanied by the choir."

Paper-clipped special in a lunch menu: Southern-Style Manhattan Clam Chowder.

Day 340

Wedding Vows

"Do you take this woman for
your wedded wife?" the minister
asked the nervous bridegroom.
"For better or worse, for richer,
for poorer, in sickness or..."

"Just a minute, Pastor!" interrupted
the bride. "Stop now, or you'll talk
him right out of it."

Day 341

Published Work

A professor was turned down
on his application to a new college
post. "Not enough published work,"
said the dean. "You have only
one book to your credit."

"Are you aware that God Himself
has only one book to His credit?"

"Then He needn't apply here."

Day 342

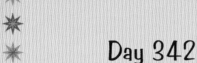

Definitions

Duffer: A golfing enthusiast who shouts "Fore!" takes five strokes, then writes three on the scorecard.

Pro Football Coach: A man who's willing to lay down his players' lives in order to win.

Quarterback: A nominal refund.

Refugee: An official at a professional wrestling match.

Day 343

Affordable Surgery

A surgeon asked a patient,
"Could you afford an operation
if I thought it was necessary?"

The patient replied, "Would you
think it was necessary if I
couldn't afford one?"

Day 344

Cinderella's Prince

Why wouldn't Cinderella
give her prince the time of day?

Because it was midnight.

Day 345

Congregational Prayer

Bobby's parents tried their best to keep him from acting up during the morning worship hour, but they were losing the battle. Finally the father picked up the little fellow and walked sternly up the aisle to apply a little discipline. Just before reaching the foyer, little Bobby called loudly to the congregation, "Pray for me! Pray for me!"

Day 346

A Long Week

Principal: "This is the fourth time you've been in my office this week. What do you have to say for yourself?"

Sam: "I'm so glad today is Friday!"

Day 347

Not Quite A+

Jeanne: "Mom, I got a hundred
in school today!"

Mom: "Good job! What did
you get a hundred in?"

Jeanne: "In two things. I got a forty
in math and a sixty in spelling."

Day 348

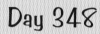

What Am I?

I come in different shapes and sizes.
Part of me has curves;
part of me is straight.
You can put me anywhere you like,
but there is only one right
place for me.
What am I?

A jigsaw puzzle.

Day 349

Better Judgment

A man was arguing with his wife over which gender shows better judgment. Ultimately, she gave in. "You're right. Men exercise better judgment, and the two of us are living proof of it, aren't we? I mean, you chose me for a wife, and I chose you for a husband."

Day 350

Pianos

Why are pianos
difficult to get into?

The keys are on the inside.

Day 351

Pianist's Note

A note left for
a pianist from his wife:

"Gone Chopin,
have Liszt, Bach in a minuet."

Day 352

- - - - - - -

Hymns

Mender's hymn: "Holy, Holy, Holy"

Politician's hymn:
"Standing on the Promises"

Shopper's hymn:
"In the Sweet By and By"

Shoe repairer's hymn:
"It Is Well with My Soul"

Librarian's hymn: "Whispering Hope"

Umpire's hymn:
"I Need No Other Argument"

Day 353

Running Commentary

A teenage couple at a movie theater
was more than conspicuous with its
audible running commentary about
the acting and the plot. At length,
a woman seated behind the couple
tapped the boy on the shoulder.

"Do you want us to ask them to turn
down the volume of the movie so you
can hear each other more clearly?"

Day 354

Phone Number

On the first day of classes,
a brash young college boy asked
the pretty girl seated next to him
for her phone number.

"It's in the phone book,"
she told him coyly.

"Under what name?" he pressed.

"That's in the book, too."

Day 355

Letter Grade

Teacher: "Jeremy, where can we find the Red Sea?"

Jeremy: "Well, there's one at the top of my last test paper."

Day 356

— — — — — — —

Things Learned in College

It doesn't matter how late you
schedule your first class—
you'll still sleep through it.

You can change so much
and barely realize it.

College kids throw airplanes, too.

If you wear polyester, everyone will ask,
"Why are you so dressed up?"

Every clock on campus shows
a different time.

Day 357

- - - - - -

What Am I?

What force and strength
cannot break through,
I with barely a touch can do.
And many in the street would wait,
Were I not a friend to the gate.
What am I?

A key.

Day 358

Worth of a Son

"How much money do
you think I'm worth, Dad?"

The father regarded his teenage son
thoughtfully. "To your mother and me,
I would say you're priceless."

"Do you think I'm worth
a thousand dollars?"

"Certainly."

"A million?"

"Even more than a million, to us."

"Would you mind giving me
about twenty of it, then?"

Day 359

Tax Consultant Advice

"Always live within your means,"
a tax consultant advised a client.

"Oh, we do," responded the client.
"We just have to take out loans
in order to do it."

Day 360

What Is It?

What word starts with *E*
and has only one letter in it?

Envelope.

Day 361

The Exact Weight

A boy was at a carnival and went to a booth where a man said to the boy, "If I write your exact weight on this piece of paper, then you have to give me fifty dollars; but if I can't, I will pay you fifty dollars."

The boy agreed, thinking no matter what the man wrote he'd just say he weighed more or less. In the end the boy ended up paying the man fifty dollars. How did the man win the bet?

The man did exactly as he said he would and wrote, "Your exact weight," on the paper.

Day 362

Murder Investigation

Two New York City detectives were investigating the murder of one Juan Flores.

"How was he killed?" asked one detective.

"With a golf gun," the other replied.

"A golf gun? What is a golf gun?"

"I don't know, but it sure made a hole in Juan!"

Day 363

Riddle Me

What do you throw out
when you need it, but take in
when you are done with it?

An anchor.

Day 364

Little League Games

Coming home from his Little League game,
Bud excitedly swung open
the front door and hollered,
"Anyone home?"

His father immediately asked,
"So how did you do, son?"

"You'll never believe it!"
Buddy announced.
"I was responsible for the winning run!"

"Really? How'd you do that?"

"I dropped the ball."

Day 365

Smarts?

I'm going to graduate on time
no matter how long it takes.

My Favorite Jokes:

My Favorite Jokes:

My Favorite Jokes:

_____

_____

_____

_____

_____

_____

_____

_____

_____

_____

My Favorite Jokes:

_____

_____

_____

_____

_____

_____

_____

_____

_____

My Favorite Jokes:

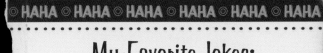

My Favorite Jokes:

My Favorite Jokes:

_____

_____

_____

_____

_____

_____

_____

_____

_____

My Favorite Jokes:

_____

_____

_____

_____

_____

_____

_____

_____

_____

_____

My Fa

My Fa

My Favorite Jokes:

_____

_____

_____

_____

_____

_____

_____

_____

My Favorite Jokes:

_____

_____

_____

_____

_____

_____

_____

_____

_____

_____

My Favorite Jokes:

_____

_____

_____

_____

_____

_____

_____

_____